A MOTHER'S LOVE

A MOVING TRIBUTE TO MY MOM

DEBANJAN ROY

Dedicated to the sacred memory of my Baba (Dad), Late Debi Prosad Roy, and Maa (Mom), Late Shubhra Roy.

Now, both of them are not here on this earth, in their physical forms.

But I have the strongest faith that they are always with me and guiding me every moment of my life.

So, it is an honour to submit my offering at their lotus feet and seek their blessings.

Contents

Prayers

God is Maa, our Divine Mother.

Maa! Homage at Your lotus feet!
Maa! Please guide us at all times!
Maa! May we ever walk on Your righteous path in life!
Maa! May we always treasure our parents!
Maa! Pranam!

Acknowledgements

To make this book possible, I am ever grateful to my Guru, Her Holiness, (late) Sri Archana Puri Maa of Sree Satyananda Devayatan, Kolkata.

Her Holiness had graced my life through the sacred 'Mantra Deeksha' (Spiritual Initiation) in 2006. Her blessings have been the continual source of my inspiration ever since I took up the pen and began writing.

Pranam at the lotus feet of my Guru!

Preface

Friends, this book you are holding in your hand is a special one indeed. It is so because its pages are dipped in the sweetest of all fragrances in this world: "a mother's love".

Stated another way, this is a book whose pages are carved out of the purest constituent in this world: the love of a mother for her son.

This is a heartfelt tribute to my mother, who left me heartbroken on 19th May 2015. And seven years have passed in the interim as I write these lines in May 2022. But to me, my mother is always there with me: she is ever-present in my heart and my memory.

A mother-son bond is the most sacred tie in the world and I firmly believe, the end of the mortal frame of my mother can never cause the dissolution of this ultra-special bond. That is because a mother's love is the direct expression of Divinity and transcends anything and everything here on this earth.

Now, in this narrative, I have intentionally left out the mention of all biographical details. Instead, I have purposely included a collage of the sweetest memories, which beautifully convey the essence of a mother's love for her son. These treasured reminiscences have so far been preserved in my heart and are being unveiled in this special memoir here.

On turning its pages, you will surely get immersed in a loving spirit of joy, that runs as the invisible current throughout. As a result, you are bound to feel rejuvenated and enriched from within.

So, the journey of love begins...

Pearls Of Love

Friends, I am now sharing some timeless pearls with you, in the form of a few beautiful quotes. These beautiful pearls will always glow bright till eternity for they represent the purest substance within: "a mother's love". So here are those pearls:

She is the only reason I am able to do what I do. - Leonardo di Caprio

Moms are guardian angels to us while they are on this earth. - Anonymous

Children and mothers never truly part. They are bound in the beating of each other's hearts. - Anonymous

My mother was the making of me. - Edison

Mother's love is bliss...it need not be acquired it need not be deserved. - Erich Fromm

There has never been, nor will there ever be, anything quite so special as the love between the mother and a son. – Anonymous

All that I am, or hope to be, I owe to my angel mother. - Abraham Lincoln

A mother's arms are made of tenderness and children sleep soundly in them. - Victor Hugo

My mother is my root, my foundation. She planted the seed that I base my life on, and that is the belief that the ability to achieve starts in your mind. – Michael Jordan

The heart of a mother is a deep abyss at the bottom of which you will always find forgiveness. – Honore de Balzac

Glossary Of Terms

Friends, while writing this account, several terms in my mother tongue of Bangla came to enter it naturally. I am placing their nearest English equivalent meanings below:

Pranam: Offering homage

Durga Puja: A sacred annual festival of Hinduism that comes in September/October

Makar Sankranti: A sacred festival of Hinduism that comes on the 14th/15th of January every year

Baba: Father

Maa: Mother

Didi: Elder Sister

Payesh: Sweet dish made of rice, milk, raisins etc.

Pitha: Sweet pancakes with the stuffing of coconut etc.

Khichuri: Preparation of rice, lentils, vegetables etc.

Vada: Fritters of vegetables

Parota and Luchi: Types of flour breads fried in oil

Begun Bhaja: A dish of fried brinjal pieces

Aloo Dum: A delicious curry of potatoes

CHAPTER I

A Loving Collage of Memories

Friends, as stated in the preface, this is a different kind of memoir. It captures the aroma of the happiest time of my life, encompassing the period from around 3 to 12 years of my age (the late-1970s to the mid-1980s). Before that, my memories are hazy and afterwards, the pressures of adolescence stole away almost all the innocent joys of life.

The main reason why I have chosen the above period is this - this slice of time represents the most beautiful interval of my life when I was a carefree boy. And this innocent boy used to just revel in the simple joys of life whilst being snugly ensconced in the radiant love of his mother. This was the most nourishing kind of love that fuelled my physical, emotional, and intellectual growth in full measure.

I wanted to express that wonderful beauty and writing afforded me that opportunity. By the Grace of God, I could hop onto a magical time machine which took me back by decades to those joyful times!

As a result, I could once again live those golden days: this led helped to start recording that blissful experience on the pages of a diary. This began just a few days after 19th May 2020, the fifth anniversary of the passing away of my Mom.

So far, these jottings have been nestling in that diary. And, now I'm sharing the indescribably affectionate flavour of that love with you because this will arouse joyous feelings within yourself too. After all, maternal love is Divine at its core.

And since a mother's love for his son is an indivisible organic whole, all I have tried is to portray just a few well-chosen memories of that ocean of bliss.

With these words, I invite you to enter the sacred realm of boundless love in the pages to follow.

CHAPTER II

Memories of Maternal Love: the Special Beauty

Friends, our childhood memories of love and affection constitute the gateway to a realm of unadulterated joy. They become a part of us, stored in the innermost alleys of our hearts and minds: we can retrieve them at will. And each time we do, they remain as fresh as ever!

And among these memories, the honour of being the sweetest and the most beautiful undoubtedly goes to the recollections of the love that we have experienced in our maternal bosom. This is because the single greatest nutrient, that nourishes the fragile sapling called 'our childhood', is the affection of our mother.

When we are growing up and experiencing our mother's love on daily basis, we often remain unaware of just how precious it is. Of course, that is not a fault on our part because then, we are still immature and we don't have any reference point. Her love seems as natural as air and sunshine to us.

Only when we reach adulthood, do we truly start realising its priceless worth. And if we are unfortunate enough to lose our mother, our appreciation of the true magnitude of her love grows a million folds.

So, in the pages that follow, you are bound to feel the fragrance of that heavenly love. And I fervently hope that you get refreshed and rejuvenated by this aroma – after all, this is the aroma with the highest possible purity in life!

CHAPTER III

Loving Memories of Home-made Food

A Mother's love:

It has been famously said that the way to a man's heart lies through his stomach. And all mothers know the truth of this statement instinctively and that's why they love to pamper their children with food!

My beloved mother was no exception to this golden rule. So, the crown of memory of my mother's love is studded with the choicest diamonds comprising remembrances of my mother's delicious cooking!

And whenever I try to analyse why her cooking lingers so fresh in my taste buds even now, I can slowly decipher the real reason. And that reason is 'a mother's love': it was the unseen yet the most important ingredient that used to lend a divine touch to even the most ordinary dish cooked by her.

So let me knowingly relive those days of unparalleled delight... I am sharing some of my fondest recollections here.

Sweet Dishes:

I just relish the memories of 'Payesh' made by Maa. It used to be my perennially beloved dish which Maa used to so lovingly prepare on many occasions. She used to especially cook it for my birthdays. That is why this dish occupies a hallowed place in my memory. Aha! What aroma it used to have! What inviting looks! What a sheer taste! The whole memory is so... so...so joyful!

And the other homemade sweet dish made by Maa was 'Pitha', the sweet coconut pancakes. She used to make them on the sacred occasion of 'Makar Sankranti' (this usually comes around January $14^{th}/15^{th}$ every year). Since this event used to come only once a year, so I used to look forward to it with great eagerness. And no store-purchased sweet dish could ever compete with this wonderful homemade preparation filled with the sweetness of maternal love!

Main Meals:

On the rainy days and during the chilly winters of Delhi, Maa used to occasionally prepare another favourite dish of mine: 'Khichuri' and 'Vada'. How yummy they used to taste! How crispy and crunchy the 'Vada' used to be! The very thought transports me to the realms of joy!

Post-school Meals:

Mother's cooking lends a golden halo to the memory of my school days in Delhi, my school being the hoary institution I revere till now: Shyama Prasad Vidyalaya Higher Secondary School. My classes here used to start at 10 AM daily and get over at 4 PM. And then my school bus used to drop me at a particular point from where I used to walk down for around 10-12 minutes to reach home.

On reaching there, Maa would lovingly scold me to wash my hands and feet and change from my school uniform to the informal home wear. But the whole of my attention used to remain geared towards the kitchen where Maa would start preparing a simple yet delicious meal for me - my choice used to be always for 'Parota' and 'Begun bhaja'. Both were fried preparations and I used to gobble them down hungrily! Aha! What joy I used to experience!

It bears mentioning that I normally avoid the fried snacks of the roadside eateries as the oil used by them is often doubtful. On the other hand, any snack prepared by Maa at home used to be my prized option. For one thing, the oil used by Maa to cook used to be very healthy. Plus the unique style of cooking used to render every dish prepared by her golden hands into a wholesome meal!

A Confession:

When I was a child, I was so accustomed to eating the daily meals made by Maa, that it would escape my attention why they tasted the way they did... I just ate them with joy...I simply took their flavours for granted.

Only on reaching adulthood (when I began cooking for myself in the hostel), I did become acutely aware of how the crucial ingredient of 'a mother's love' used to make such a huge difference to any dish!

Oh! I miss the loving touch of Maa so much!

CHAPTER IV

Loving Memories of Hand-woven Clothing

The Silent Touch:

After the diamonds described in the previous chapter, I come to the rubies of my memory of the touch of clothing. This constitutes another golden instance of love and affection of Maa for me.

Maa used to knit quite a lot when I was a child and the feeling of wearing any piece of her knitwear is something that cannot be expressed in words - it can only be felt in the psyche of a 5-year-old child. Some tidbits of those indescribable feelings are shared below:

Just the other day while I was writing this memory in May 2020, I chanced to espy several plastic wrappers. On opening, these wrappers revealed quite a few woollen balls stored within. These were wools in various shades: when I chose to examine them, I gradually got dissolved in a flood of tears! That's because, despite the passage of nearly 40 years, I could instantly recognise the deep red shade of one of those wools.

And I was taken back by a time machine into the golden period of my childhood: I could see myself being taken to the famous Buddha Jayanti Park in Delhi on a school picnic - I was then most probably studying Class 2 in my School, Shyama Prasad Vidyalaya in Delhi - I saw myself sitting on the window seat of our school bus, sporting a bright red full sleeve sweater on an equally bright sunny day of the winter.

As I wrote these lines, there began to arise such lovely feelings within me: I could slowly feel the warm cosiness imparted by the soft touch of that woollen wear! And I could smell the aroma of that sweater so lovingly knitted by Maa! How secure I felt inside that sweater on that day 40 years ago! What a cosy feeling I could relive once more! What a bliss it was!

Of course, the ready-to-wear sweaters purchased in the market have got far more intricate designs and much better variations in colour. But despite such qualities, they can never match the joy of wearing a sweater hand-knitted by Maa!

The reason definitely lies in the silent maternal affection - the invisible thread – that ties all such hand-knitted clothing. And when I used to wear such a cloth, then that love used to get equally silently transferred on to me. No words can ever verbally describe that divine love, which gets transmitted from a mother onto her son, in myriads of such unseen ways!

The Festive Season:

I strongly remember the chilly winters of Delhi - they produce a glow of warmth within me now - I simply get bathed in the memory of the maternal care associated with this beautiful season! The cold season usually started to descend on Delhi from the month of October. That used to coincide with the joyous season hosting the favourite festival among Bengalis: the celebrations of Durga Puja!

I fondly remember that the whole family – Baba, Maa, Didi and myself used to love attending the night long cultural extravaganza organised as a part of Puja celebrations at the CR Park locality of Delhi; we used to return home only at dawn the next day and it used to be quite chilly at that point in time. It is during these occasions that motherly affection used to be showered on me in full measure: Maa used to always carry a half sleeve sweater for me in her bag. As a mark of her concern for me, she used to make me wear that sweater at the time of our return home. I dimly recall I used to protest but to no avail!

A Strict Regimen:

During our stay in Delhi, both November and February used to have very pleasant cold weather. December and January, however, used to be bitterly cold. Maa had prescribed a strict protocol of warm clothing for me in this season. I recall she used to knit both half and full sweaters for me. I used to wear the former during October-November and February – March periods. And then I used to wear both kinds during the December-January season. And when the minimum temperature at night used to fall to the low of 4 degrees Celsius at the height of winter, I had to wear two half sweaters beneath the full sweater.

This entire episode is a standing symbol of the thorough care and love Maa used to bestow on me in her own way. During that time, as a boy, I used to grumblingly comply with her dictum...then I used to mind all these impositions (as I saw them) so much!

Now, as an adult what an afterglow of joy these memories produce in my mind! This is especially so because I have started realising the extent of motherly care and concern for me! How exhilarating it feels to recall such sweet memories now!

Oh, Maa! I miss you so much!

CHAPTER V

Loving Memories of Special Routines

Maa used to display her care for me in umpteen ways!

One such special way flashed in my memory while writing the previous chapter on my clothing regimen in the winters of Delhi. And that is the memory of my special bath routines during the same season. When the climate in Delhi used to turn bitterly cold, then this system laid down by Maa used to come into effect. It had its own special nuances!

For example, one day I used to take bath in warm water and the next day I was allowed to forego it. How happy I used to feel on that day when I could get away by just sponging myself! Now, to someone unfamiliar with the bitingly cold weather of December-January in the northern plains of India, this system may seem a bit odd. But I used to frankly look forward to such bath-less days!

That's because taking bath used to be such a challenge to me then: the initial warmth of the water used to soon fall near the room temperature - pouring the first mug of that semi-cold water on my naked and shivering body used to be such a struggle! And taking off multiple layers of warm clothing for a bath lasting hardly a few minutes and then putting on those many layers back again used to be so cumbersome! So, I used to be just thankful for the alternate days when I could escape with just a body sponge! Anyone who has lived in the cold weather of winter in North India can empathise with what I've written here.

All these memories bring such a pleasant glow to my mind now!

CHAPTER VI

Loving Memories of Forming Good Habits

Rightly it has been said that habits can either make or mar our lives. That's why our parents are so strict about ensuring that we should start adopting good habits right from childhood. And, once such virtuous habits become ingrained into our inner being, then we continue to reap their amazingly beneficial fruits all through our lives. Maa was no exception to this rule: that is why I feel so grateful now... the regime of strict habits I formed under her care is continuing to stand by me even now.

One such cluster of habits pertains to the vital area of health and hygiene. Here, Maa used to show her abundant concern for me by making me follow strict habits of personal cleanliness. For example, I had to compulsorily wash my hands with soap and thoroughly wash my legs with water every time I used to step into the threshold of our home from the road outside. I also had to mandatorily wash my hands before eating anything. And the washing of legs was a must before climbing onto the bed every night. Ahh! What a rigid protocol of habits I had to follow then!

Another area where Maa used to put her foot down heavily was the obligatory discipline of washing any utensil such as a plate, bowl spoon or glass before using it for eating or drinking. Normally when I used to feel thirsty at the height of summer in our Delhi home, my first impulse would be to just grab a glass, pour water into it and start drinking straight away. But no! Maa would strictly disallow any such thing! She used to insist that I should first wash that glass with water before using it to drink.

In the same manner, when I used to feel ravenously hungry after returning home from school, my initial instinct would be to grab just any plate lying in front of me and place the foodstuff on it. This was again a strict no-no for Maa. She would frown upon any such impetuous action and insist on washing my plate with water first - only then I was allowed to keep any eatable upon it.

At that point of immaturity in my childhood, often I used to protest and grumble, "Maa, you are just too much! Why do I have to wash my hands and legs so many times? And why should I wash my plate and glass each time?" But Maa would have none of it and I had no choice but fall in line with her system. And since then, these habits have got entrenched in me.

After the passage of so many decades, I came to recognise afresh the tremendous significance of what Maa has done for me, at the time of writing this memoir in May 2020. It was the height of mayhem caused by the corona pandemic and then everyone, right from the Prime Minister down to doctors, was sternly advising the citizens of India to wash their hands repeatedly!

Ah! In a flash, I could discern the boundless wisdom of Maa and her deep-seated love for me that had made me from such stupendously good habits of hygiene early in life... they have stood the test of time so well...and they were simply life-savers for me during the corona outbreak!

Maa, you are just like a guardian angel!

This was certainly true while your blissful presence was there with me. And even now, from your heavenly perch, you are taking care of me!

Maa, pranam at your lotus feet!

CHAPTER VII

Loving Memories of Self Discipline and Hard Toil of Maa

Self-discipline and hard work are those invisible yet extraordinarily powerful catalysts which make everything in life possible. They are thus equivalent to God in the life of man. And it was Maa, the representative of God on earth, who had instilled these virtues in my character right from my childhood. Most of this invisible process took place by example as Maa was the epitome of self-discipline and industriousness herself. As a result, these golden qualities got transmitted from mother to son as part of a wonderful learning protocol. An apt illustration is portrayed below.

My school used to start at 10 AM and the school bus used to arrive at 9 AM to pick me up. The bus route was so designed that it used to pick me up almost the first in the morning. Now, this pickup point was quite a distance from home and I used to walk around 10-12 minutes to reach it - so I had to get ready and start from home by 8:40 AM or so every single day.

Maa, being self-disciplined, used to wake up early in the morning daily and immediately start toiling hard for her family. And slowly I also began imbibing the same welcome traits in my character by example: I habitually started getting up in the morning, completing morning studies, packing my school bag with the right books, stationery, tiffin box and so on ... everything on time.

In the evening my school used to get over at 4 PM and then my school bus used to drop me at the same spot.

And after walking home, my evening routine of meals, play, study etc. used to start ... again everything used to be completed in a timely manner, thanks to the constant sacrifices made by Maa. This was just an illustration. And there are so many other instances to share.

So, Maa had to be well-organized and slog for me from morning till evening every day to ensure that my own academic life should go on smoothly and at an even pace. She had to thus remain on her toes just for my sake.

Oh, Maa! How much you toiled for me all through your life! What wonderful examples you set for me!

Whatever I could achieve in life is only because of Maa...!

Maa, I bow down to you!

CHAPTER VIII

Loving Memories of School Life

In the life of any growing child, his school and studies come to occupy the lion's share. In my case also this phase of life occupies a special place in my heart. And in the centre of that stands Maa – her invaluable role in moulding my academic life is simply beyond any description. In the paragraphs below, I try to just share a glimpse.

Homework:

I fondly recall how strict Maa was in the most important part of my school-life: my studies. She used to ensure that I should complete all my homework in a timely and neat manner. Initially, she used to keep a strict tab on this: slowly I got into the virtuous habit of keeping myself always up to date in each of the subjects taught in class during school hours. As a result, I could easily answer any question asked by my subject teacher in his/her next class. And this also used to help me remain well prepared for any surprise test in the class.

Academic Success in Exams:

I would now like to gratefully touch upon the thoroughness of Maa's coaching for the exams in my school.

In this context, I would like to appreciate the rigorous internal evaluation system of my beloved school, Shyama Prasad Vidyalaya and commend the school authorities for instituting this system: - in each academic year from May to April, there used to be four compulsory exams: 1st term, 2nd term, 3rd term and then, Finals in September, December, February and April respectively.

And it is my privilege to declare that it was solely Maa's blessing that brought sustained success in my academic life: I could top every single term exam consecutively from Class III to Class X in school! It was she who transferred the qualities of sincerity and diligence to me. It is due to her excellent coaching I grew the lifetime habit of regular study, completion of syllables well in time and not keeping anything pending till the last moment. Hence, the full credit goes to Maa.

So, I proudly state that Maa was 100% responsible for all my achievements - my own contribution was simply 0% here. All I used to do is just blindly follow the discipline laid down by her: good results used to follow inevitably!

Some More Tidbits:

An important aspect of the school was my uniform which had to be compulsorily worn there every day. If I recall correctly, my summer uniform used to comprise the white shirt, white trousers, white socks, and black shoes. Later on, a maroon tie was made a part of this attire. And in winter, this uniform used to change to the grey sweater, white shirt and matching grey trousers.

Everyone familiar with Delhi knows how dusty it is especially in the summers. So, to properly maintain a white uniform in such weather is a challenging proposition indeed. But Maa used to take care that my uniform should be spotlessly white while Baba used to iron them. In this manner, my loving parents used to ensure that I was freshly geared up for school every working day.

Maa also used to pack my tiffin box daily. And eating that simple yet delicious meal during the tiffin hour in school used to be so pleasurable... it used to keep me reminded of Maa even during school hours!

Tribute:

Today is 19th May 2022 - the 7th death anniversary of my Maa. And as I read and revise the above lines for writing the final version of this chapter, my mind keeps repeatedly going back to those golden years. The sweet pictures of my school, my teachers (I'm so grateful to each one of them), my classmates, my school bus, my exams, my projects... keep blessing my memory.

And towering above them all stands the lighthouse of love and care of Maa: a love that is as boundless as the deepest ocean on this earth!

My pranam at the lotus feet of Maa!

CHAPTER IX

Loving Memories of Leisure Time

Pressed by the relentless rigours of academic life, a child always longs for respite. That welcome break is afforded by Sundays, the blessed day when he is relatively free and thus can enjoy his life a bit more. Here also Maa's contributions stand supreme in making my leisure hours on Sundays to be so blissful!

My beloved school, Shyama Prasad Vidyalaya used to function from Monday to Saturday and Sunday used to be the off day. Many years later Saturday also got added to this welcome list of weekly off! So, after attending school continuously from 10 AM to 4 PM for 6 days a week, I used to naturally look forward to Sundays. And the first bonus of this beautiful day was: - I was allowed to wake in the morning a bit later than the weekdays. This was a special bonus indeed!

Then it used to be the turn of the next prize: the Sunday breakfast! My favourite menu was the vegetable chowmein prepared so deliciously by Maa. How keenly I used to wait for the treat! For a boy like me, eating a piping hot dish of chowmein topped by a dash of tomato ketchup was a truly delectable pleasure, to be savoured at leisure! The relaxed Sunday lunch eaten in the company of Baba and Didi, followed by an afternoon siesta, was the other hallmarks of my Sunday routine.

Watching TV for a longer duration was another privilege allowed to me only on Sundays - both Baba and Maa used to be very strict about this aspect on the weekdays. Since class VII, I had begun wearing spectacles and so, while watching TV, I had to follow strict rules: I had to keep eight feet distance away from the TV and I could not watch TV duration for more than thirty-forty minutes at a stretch.

The only golden exception was the Sunday evening when we as a whole family used to gather together in the living room and watch the Hindi feature film telecast by Doordarshan, the sole channel on TV. Many a time, these films used to turn out to be run of the mill type and not very attractive to watch. Yet all these minuses used to get over-ruled by the indescribable sense of joy and security experienced by me in sitting together with Baba, Maa and Didi for that duration of two and half hours and enjoying the warmth of such once-in-a-week family gatherings.

Alas! Now that Baba and Maa are no more, the memory of those distant evenings has come to acquire such a nostalgic connotation that it cannot be expressed in words! Only someone who has experienced the loss of parents can perceive my agony!

Baba, Maa! How much I miss both of you!

CHAPTER X

Loving Memories of Hobbies

Our hobbies play a very important role in our lives. This is especially true in our childhood when everything in this world gives joy to us: our hobby then provides a valuable outlet through which our creative imagination finds free expression. Such creativity becomes a source of authentic happiness and begins to boost our self-esteem significantly - its positive effects soon start flowing over into academics and other parts of our lives, with beneficial results all around.

This is what that had happened in my case also. Since my earliest childhood, I had been very fond of reading - the term 'bookworm' can be easily applied to me. This hobby used to take roots even stronger during the summer vacations when we would be making our cherished visit to my maternal home Dhanbad - I used to simply devour all the storybooks I could find there! And due to this, my creative streak got bolstered - this used to help me a lot in my studies as well as in my other hobby of drawing and painting.

Here again, I'm grateful to Maa because I could balance my studies and my hobbies due to the wonderful system of self-discipline that she had instilled in me. My reading habit also got strengthened due to her insistence on my studying the school textbooks thoroughly.

However, for preserving the health of my eyesight, Maa used to insist that I give my eyes a rest after reading storybooks for some time. And she would ask me to keep all of them in one place so that I can easily find them when needed next time. For this purpose, she had assigned me a black iron chest.

Aha! What fond associations are there with that chest because as a child, it was nothing short of a treasure trove for me! That chest is indeed a cherished part of so many beautiful memories! And the reason was it used to contain all my favourite books: books of stories, books of comics, books of children's literature, books of fairy tales, and so on.

Throughout my boyhood, I used to love lifting the cover of the chest, taking out a book at random and just enjoying the feel of the book. I particularly used to like the distinctive aroma that comes out on opening the covers of an old but well-preserved book. All book lovers will agree that such an aroma is as good as heaven for a certified bookworm!

Maa, I'm just so grateful to you! You have nurtured the seeds of the reading habit within me, a habit that has given me so much happiness all through my life and does so even now as I write this joyful memoir of a joyful hobby!

CHAPTER XI

Loving Memories of Family Travels

Our childhood travels in the company of one's loving family always remain a source of enormously pleasurable memory for us when we grow up. That's because, what looks commonplace to a world-weary adult mind such as a railway station, is an absolute marvel in the eyes of a child! And during such travels with his family, he comes to relish all the unique sights, sounds, smells, tastes and touches that can only be found in a typical journey, especially on a journey by train on the vast network of Indian Railways.

This is particularly true for my childhood travels in the 1970s and the 1980s: that was the time when steam locomotives could still be found huffing and puffing on our tracks...they used to seem a grand sight indeed to the curious mind of a child...how joyous all those memories are for me!

Let me now present some tidbits of those memories here. On the screen of my mind, I can see the flashback to those glorious days when we would be making our annual trips to my paternal home at Calcutta and maternal home at Dhanbad. My school used to close for summer vacations during May - June and Baba used to accordingly book our tickets for travel to Kolkata by New Delhi-Howrah Deluxe Express in May. I used to so excitedly look forward to our journey when I could gorge on my second favourite pastime (reading of course came first...!) of trains: I used to just love riding a train as well as watching other trains whizz by.

Aha! How pleasurable my journeys onboard Deluxe Express used to be in the company of my Baba, Maa, and Didi! And among all delights, the prime object of my interest would be the big tiffin carrier: it would be containing my ever-favourite dishes of 'Luchi' and 'Aloo Dum'. These delicious items used to be cooked by Maa on the morning of our journey date and constituted one of the best combinations of dishes in my eyes! Just how much I used to enjoy that loving touch of Maa during those travels! And I have to confess that I have tasted these very dishes so many times later on in my life but nothing can even come close to the memory of those delicious train dinners! And it is all because of the magic touch of Maa!

In my life, later on, I have undertaken so many journeys by so many diverse means of transport: bus, train, aeroplane etc...but without the graceful presence of Maa, they all lacked that element of vitality that used to animate my childhood travels on trains and make them so joyful.

Maa! I miss you everywhere!

CHAPTER XII

Homage to Maa

Freinds, just like precious pearls, so many nuggets of golden memories of Maa are preserved within my inner being. For me, they are simply priceless!

Such gems, hidden in the deep recesses of my mind, often come to me in momentary flashes and provide me with solace in the hours of grief when the pangs of separation from Maa become too intense to bear.

In the foregoing pages, I have tried to retrieve some of them and bring them to light. As you will appreciate, the lion's share of these jewels is in the form of transcendent feelings. So, only a little could be documented through words in black and white. The pages that I could chronicle are my modest homage to her lotus feet.

And I discovered that penning down the cherished memories of Maa was so soothing and at the same time, such a deeply painful experience. While I was absorbed in writing, it was so joyous to relive those blissful days spent in the enchanted circle of maternal love, a love which is unquestionably the purest in this entire world. Through such nostalgic flashbacks, I could transport myself back to those idyllic days!

At the same time, this process was so...so...so painful! It went on giving me sharp jabs of anguish as I perceived the physical absence of Maa afresh again and again. I felt like breaking into loud sobs which I have done many times in the past since Maa left me heartbroken in 2015. And I continue to do so when the agony of separation from her loving presence becomes too strong!

With these heartfelt words, I am bringing my pen to a halt here - I am simply unable to articulate my sentiments anymore - such emotions can only be experienced by a deeply reverential heart!

Maa! I miss you so much!

Pranam to Maa!

Printed by Libri Plureos GmbH in Hamburg, Germany